AFTER

Books by Robert Gibb

Sheet Music (Autumn House Press, 2012)

The Empty Loom (University of Arkansas Press, 2012)

What the Heart Can Bear (Autumn House Press, 2009)

World over Water (University of Arkansas Press, 2007)

The Burning World (University of Arkansas Press, 2004)

The Origins of Evening (W.W. Norton & Co., 1998)

Fugue for a Late Snow (University of Missouri Press, 1993)

Momentary Days (Walt Whitman Center, 1989)

The Winter House (University of Missouri Press, 1984)

The Names of the Earth in Summer (Stone Country, 1983)

AFTER

POEMS

Robert Gibb

MARSH HAWK PRESS
East Rockaway, New York • 2017

7 6 5 4 3 2 1 FIRST EDITION

Marsh Hawk Press books are published by Poetry Mailing List, Inc., a not-for-profit corporation under section 501(c)3 United States Internal Revenue Code.

Book Design: Susan Quasha
cover art: © 2017 Gillian Widden (www.gillianwidden.com)
The teasel is called Dipsacus fullonum

Library of Congress Cataloging-in-Publication Data

Names: Gibb, Robert, 1946- author.
Title: After : poems / by Robert Gibb.
Description: East Rockaway : Marsh Hawk Press, 2017.
Identifiers: LCCN 2016035610 | ISBN 9780996427562 (pbk)
Classification: LCC PS3557.I139 A6 2017 | DDC 811/.54--dc23 LC record
available at https://lccn.loc.gov/2016035610

Marsh Hawk Press
P.O. Box 206
East Rockaway, New York 11518-0206
www.marshhawkpress.org

ACKNOWLEDGEMENTS

Brilliant Corners: "Winter Concert," "Saying Goodbye," "Listening to Pharoah Sanders: A Poem For My Son On His Birthday"

Gettysburg Review: "Winter Thaw, Monongahela River, New Homestead, Pennsylvania"

Great River Review: "New Homestead Sequence," "Arboretum," "Feeding the Deer," "Stacking the Fire," "Westinghouse Memorial Pond"

Green Linden: "Cardinal, Cardinal," "Work Song," "Water Garden: Lock & Dam"

Green Mountains Review: "The Writing on the Wall"

The Hudson Review: "River Light"

The Kenyon Review: "After"

Lake Effect: "Funeral Rites"

Long Pond Review: "Nearing Winter"

Meridian: "Wildflowers (II)," "Snow Days"

The New Yorker: "Hummingbird"

Notre Dame Review: "Joining the Debate," "Plant Profile"

Paper Streets: "Street Market, February"

Poetry: "On Not Telling Anyone at the Bar"

Poetry Ireland Review: "Spring Sequence"

Poetry Northwest: "Reading Keats in Frick Park During the First Weeks of Spring"

Prairie Schooner: "April Journal," Widower," "Two Songs," "Against Transcendence," "Road Signs," "Late Hours," "Cathay"

Sequoia: "Epilogue"

Snail's Pace Review: "Teasel"

The Southern Review: "Take Another Look," "Specimen Days,"
   "Moths," "Wildflowers (I)," "Endgame in August"
Strand Magazine: "Larry""
The Threepenny Review: "Aphasia"
"Against Transcendence" and "Road Signs" were part of a group of poems
given *Prairie Schooner*'s Strousse Award for 2010.

"Late Hours" was also a *Poetry Daily* selection.

for Maggie

CONTENTS

I

II

III

here have we fixed our dwelling
after our sorrow
            —POUND, CANTO LIII

I

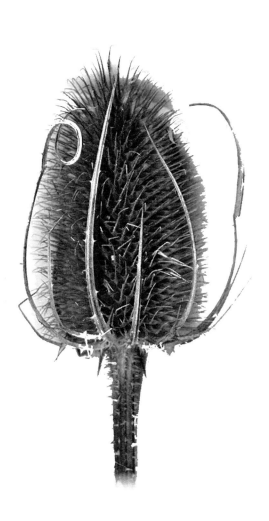

READING KEATS IN FRICK PARK
DURING THE FIRST WEEKS OF SPRING

Once again, the old trees in the park:

The great oaks and locusts twisting upward
Into the green fire of their crowns,

And the dogwoods which were smoke all winter,
The beeches which were columns of stone.

Sunlight the honey now ticking in the limbs.

It's summer already on the cover
Of Keats's letters, judging by the lushness

Of Constable's trees, though inside
I've left him to that chill, Devon spring

He complains of, a few months from the Lakes

And Scotland—the walking tours
On which he'll rack the lining of his lungs.

Even now he's been listening to rain
with a sense of being drown'd, rotted

like a grain of wheat, as if such jest

Were foreshadowing, which it's made to seem,
His life plotted out like a novel.

Still to come are those *plaguy* sore throats,
The *awful warmth* about the heart

He confused with immortality.

Nor did truth turn out to be any urn of beauty
But its own. And yet these days

The world seems a lot like the one in his ode,
Freed from the yearly round

And *unwearied* there: budding air, lovers

Strolling together beneath the *leaf-fring'd* trees
They believe will never grow bare.

And so it must appear, knobbed shoots
Sprouting on the ginkgoes,

Blossoms spotting in the cherries' boughs.

THE WRITING ON THE WALL

Beyond the felt-green lawns of the bowlers, on
A path just inside the park, I found it: *Verse*,

Set in cursive among the other names sprayed upon
The stones, yet with none of their swollen letters,

Iridescent as molds.
                              Solitary and light,
It floated in the shadows like a blossom

At the spread end of the bough. But whether
It was meant as a subject or summons

Or was the tag someone chose to be known by,
There was no way for me to tell.
                                        A year later,

Traced over, it shone a rust-stained red
From the stones. Scoured by weather, the acids

Of the city air, it's now grown fainter still,
Leaving the wall with nothing but its riddle.

TAKE ANOTHER LOOK

1. *Snapshot*

A young woman posed before the front of a trolley
Hung on a chain link fence, their backdrop

The tavern's grottoed patio in which people sit.
Picnic tables. Uprights of an arbor

Canopied with still-bare vines. The worn scroll
On the trolley reads HOMESTEAD-DUQUESNE,

Brackets for a stretch of track, the woman's clothes
Dating from decades after it lapsed,

The claret of her jacket matching the fleur-de-lys
You've noticed speckling her indigo dress.

Most likely it's the promise of grapes in the photo
That has you now studying her wild black hair

And how it's touched at the top with sunlight,
A little crown of tendrils on fire.

The wrought-iron shadows filigreed beside her,
The light coming level from the right ...

All clues to the season and time of day,
Though the occasion remains opaque—memorial

Or spur-of-the-moment? Take another look.
Peripheral, you're still drawn in by the scene,

The way that man is, sitting alone in the background,
Staring straight into the lens.

2. *Backstory*

Camera put away, my wife and I sat in the patio
The way we did on summer afternoons,

Grapes straight out of Caravaggio
Hanging above us, filtering the light,

The sound of a slow freight in the distance
Keeping rhythm, and ample time

For another round. Clouded purple clusters.
Bees like flecks of the honeyed sun.

When she died, I had the bar at least for solace.
Then, before long, not even that.

Only an empty space where the air in summer
Wavers above the pavement.

Weeks after he'd sold it, we'd see the old man
Sitting alone out back (who'd thought

He wanted nothing to survive him),
Trapped in the wreckage of what he'd done.

3. *Another Look*

And if that trolley had read DESIRE?
Could this be anything to you but oddment,

Snapshot, a moment's coalescence
In which the light has been stopped?

The coppery crown-fire of the tendrils,
The thorn of the sun in her hair …

You're hardly at fault. The occasions of grief,
After all, are absent from the photograph,

Except for the late-day shadows
Which are synoptic for us all.

ON NOT TELLING ANYONE AT THE BAR

At first because it was nobody else's business.
Then because we needed a place where the ordinary

Held sway, unlorded by lab-work and x-rays,
The long odds offered by the doctors.
                               And finally,

Because I could not find a place for her death there
In the auspices of gossip, small talk, and jokes,

I cast her absence as boredom with our blather.
Whenever they asked about her, it was one more jolt.

I sat there, Ash Wednesday, after saying goodbye,
Wondering how to tell our children,
                               trying to shake

My way free of the vision of her bleeding away,
Head strapped in the halo of the aspirator's brace.

At the bar a forehead with its thumb-smudged cross.
Ashes like the urn-full I'd bring home in a box.

FUNERAL RITES

i.

William Carlos Williams thought
His neighbors should know how
To perform a funeral and be worthy
Of their grief, which was ritual,
Communal, a matter of the weather
Into which they walked, his tract
Taking shape among them.
Years later, all the hopes he'd held
For them came to rest in the body
Of that sparrow escutcheoned upon
The pavement, having done its best.
How like him to have singled out
The common coin of the flock,
Casting his elegies in a major key.
Cortège, plumed word, stripped bare
Of its trappings. No gilt wheels
And no wreathes either. Only
The planed raw beauty of the grain.

ii.

That last scene in *Being There*, before
The credits start to roll: the fool
Strolls off on his own from the funeral

And knowing no better, walks upon
The water his dipstick umbrella
Can't fully plumb. It's fathomless,
But then so is the path across it
And the way he won't either sink
Or swim. The allusion's obvious,
Though no one in the movie sees him.
Nor, unlike the disciples, are any of us
Approached by the miraculous.
The figure on the pond's moving off,
To be replaced by the actor
Who keeps slipping out of character
In the outtakes behind the credits,
Disbelief suddenly changing sides,
The audience bearing witness.

JOINING THE DEBATE

i.

In John McGahern's story, "The Wine Breath,"
The quarrel concerning the English
And Latin Mass becomes a debate
About the "common" and "proper" names of flowers,

As one priest's framed it, arguing in favor
Of the latter, Linnaean, catholic names,
While his friend intones the litany
Of "dog rose, wild woodbine, buttercup, daisy ... "

ii.

And yet Adam didn't name the animals in Latin, I think,
looking up from the page. Nor were the trees in the garden
fitted out with brass-tag taxonomies. Again this evening
I watched our front-yard ornamental fade in the grainy light—
branches I've seen dissolve in darkness since our first days
here. I'd paged through the field guide, looking for the oak-
lobed leaves and shagbark-hickory trunk, the seeds on their
airy spindles, but none of them were in it. And that meant
a visit to the reference stacks, checking among paragraphs
and plates, to at last discover the listing for *paper maple*
and with it the brace of trochees that made the tree replete.

iii.

To set against the sway of species and genus
A bouquet of names on the breath.

APRIL JOURNAL

Wild turkeys on the lawn again today. They come in like
cindery planets, gaunt looking, black with rain, before
erupting into their colors, patch-quilt and back-dropped
with fans. They face off, broadside, or sidle past each other,
dark inflamed dynasts ignored by the foraging hens.

*

Audubon, like Franklin, gave them pride of place among
our native birds.

*

April—"cruelest," "shoures soote"—from the Old French
avrill and the Latin *aprillis.* Syllables like grit for the gizzard.

*

My friend's wildcatting Irish father, late of Bakersfield
and its oil rigs, turned mystic toward the end of his life,
reading *Magister Ludi* and throwing the *I Ching* each night,
divining what the next day held in store, which one day
was his death. He finessed it for a time, his journals show,
by backdating the entries—hexagrams stacked neatly
as cairns above each written note—beginning in media res
all over again, having come late into his April.

*

A late spring snow, against which I've tented the tomatoes,
bivouacking the rows.

*

Roosting among the cell-phone panels at the top of the mast,
where I've seen vultures sitting out a November rain,
that squat black shape fans his tail and turns into a turkey,
alone on a ceiling up hundreds of feet. A crow's-nest rigged
above the trees. At some point he'll be crashing back down,
feathers flying, like a bushel basket filled with leaves.
And the image for his earlier ascent? Cargo, maybe, hoisted
by a davit, or something gusting suddenly up the chimney?

*

The toad out back in the garden, a beaded clod dislodged
by my hoe.

*

The turkeys in regalia.

NEW HOMESTEAD SEQUENCE

1. Paper Streets

streets which exist only in municipal records
    —PITTSBURGH POST-GAZETTE

True places, said Melville, are never on the map.
Take, for example, the Lot & Block's pictured
In the pages of the New Homestead Plan.
You can see them down at Deeds and Records
Like templates for the impending world
Whose paper streets are real: a phantom ward,
Scaled and canted, the ink now faded to taupe.
It never got off the drawing-board.

Here, where spirit levels hung and surveyors
Set their sights, those thoroughfares unfurl—
Lanes for wild pear and chokecherry, corridors
Through which the great-keeled turkeys wade.
Cock birds on the lawns are our peacocks,
But wattled, iridescent in their plush brocade.

2. Owls on the Summer Solstice

They were like something ornamental
Set into the trees, saw-whet and fledgling,
Their raspy hisses filling the air,

Loud enough to bring me out of the house
And find parts of the woods gathered there.
Even with a full moon it was hard
To see them clearly, back-lit and sentinel,
The size of an upheld hand.
Almost motionless at first, they looked back
From a darkness diffuse with light
Candled in the cones of their eyes.
The big owls feed on hawks, I thought,
But these seemed almost comic,
Their beaks and talons impossible to make out,
Their little heads on swivels.
Then one broke from its branch and floated—
Silent, enormous—
Through air its wings never stirred.
Something peripheral, glimpsed in a bird.

3. *Signs & Wonders*

First, that loud startled cluck and the sound
Of the turkey walloping up into the tree.
(I was busy hoeing weeds.)
Then, as I was thinking how impossible

Their flight always seems,
Out from the underbrush came something
More impossible still. Its head-down,
Lolling, tongue-out trot froze me

On the spot. Fox-like, but twice the size,
So intent on the scent it never noticed me,
I watched the coyote quicken the air
At the bottom of my yard

Where the mown grass smells like corn silk.
Rangy, emphatic, it prowled wilder
By half than our own deer and turkeys—
Animals the tomcat mostly ignores.

The other day, after it had stormed,
Blossoms from the silk trees
Covered the lawns with rainbows.
It brought us an abundance like that.

4. *The River of Heaven*

Flower clusters in the trees like tied dry flies:
Claret Bumble, Peacock Lady, Pale Evening Dun.

5. *Rabbit Ode*

And to feel the light is a rabbit-light,
In which everything is meant for you
      — WALLACE STEVENS

Who can blame him for wanting to burrow
Under fragrant clouds of thyme,

The vegetable beds all tended, the silk trees
Unfurling their ferny leaves?

The best time of year, as I've told my son,
When nothing has yet gone wrong

And even the rabbit seems to belong
To a plenitude, like the light's.

Burrow filled in, I check along the fence,
Hoping he'll be luckier than last year's

Jumpy visitor who wound up tangled in it.
I'd thought he'd be loose in a minute

And so kept my distance, not wanting
To alarm him more. I needn't have.

He'd been dead for at least the night,
The head and neck gnawed completely off,

The rest of him ropy, strung up in the wire.
I waited for weeks for the air to clear

Of all the ghosts he'd left hanging there.
Now he's back in the flesh as if resident

For the long run of summer days
He'll dig into, if I let him.

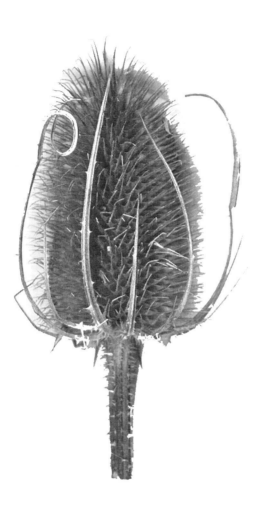

SPECIMEN DAYS

i.

Dwarfs & Bonsai: *Japanese Courtyard,*
Phipps Conservatory

It has no garden, I remember, the heart
Of Rilke's dwarf. But here, among floral ships-

In-a-bottle, these buckled lovers stroll, arm
In arm, looking up at laptop Cypress

And Chinese Elms, fruiting Pomegranate—
Trunks like twisted strands of mop or riddled

Coral stands, nickel gravel for boulders
And shrubs of lichen moss. Rain's left puddles

Among them, ponds it's easy to imagine
Stocked with small red carp.
                                        Art or nature,

Which one holds the mirror? And what is meant
By full-grown here?
                                Up the path, before

The pagodas where the lovers have stopped,
Sculpted water churns through rock.

ii.

Desert Storm: *Metal Sculpture,*
Carnegie Museum of Art

In its flat, sectioned, Samurai plates, tail
Bent above it like a back hoe, the scorpion

Is still no match for the "single organism"
The ants become, even with one impaled

On its stinger.
                    The swarm, configured here
In five soldered bodies tipped with prongs

And bent-metal antennae, storms up the pincers
Off the marble floor: a pinioned throng

In this parable of battle, hardly more
Inanimate than insects seem for real—
                                their steel

Braised with copper, scorches from the torch.
Within a few minutes you can almost feel

The numb, going-under of the scorpion,
The filings-to-magnet clamp of the ants.

iii.

Hornworms: *Community Gardens,*
Homewood Cemetery

Plush upholstered hungers slung along
The undersides of stems on which they hung

Feasting, we searched for them nightly,
Parting plants like waters,
                              peering into that welter

For horned, green motley slashed with white
And serrated to their leaves.

They start from the eggs, from the earth,
Clutching their slow way upward,
                              casting scat

Like round gray seeds beneath the plants.
In another life they rose on mothwings—

Hawk, Sphinx, Hummingbird—
Soft as the dusks in which they sought out nectar.

Here they're nearly chlorophyll,
Plucked from trusses, crushed beneath the heel.

MOTHS

i.

Morning, the brown moth mantling on the deck rail—
A fluttering slip of bark lifted from its tree.

Seen at a distance the wings are like veneer
Marbled with tan and umber and burnt-sienna bands,

But when I get closer they're almost powdery,
Nothing more than dust. Nothing, these mornings,
I'm likely to parse, though this is lexical as well, *moth*

and rust, a mummified bundle, borne aloft.

ii.

Again this morning I've been listening to the chirring
Of these moths in their mating flights

And watching how the wing patches, flat lime-white,
Flash their semaphores across the leafy air.

Then the flex of the resting bodies. I've been thinking
About that desk in the funeral home,
Her obituary on it like a scissored swatch of cloth—

A garment, wrote the psalmist, *fretted by moths*.

HUMMINGBIRD

i.

Shunt and plumb bob, a whirring top
That keeps touching down on its pivot.

The cambered wings, *like blurry gauze,*
And the long, thin, nectar-threading bill

Of a bird that backs off only to start again
From its still point in midair.

The revved-up, head-first metabolism.
The stone at the throat like a heart.

ii.

High in the Altiplano, its wings spread
Hundreds of feet across, a hummingbird
Flies among the other sky-faced drawings
The Nazca paced off on their tarmac.

iii.

Walk me through something like that.

WILDFLOWERS (I)

i.

Hawkweed and chicory along the roadsides,
Gall-of-the-earth beneath the trees,

The path through the woods walled with sun-
Flowers—yellow rays floating on the green,

Upright ply of leaves, eight- to ten-feet tall—
The stippled clouds of joe-pye among them,

And ironweed now coming into blossom,
Its deep-inked purples jolting the light.

ii.

A bank of buttercups transfixed us once as boys.
Then we were preempted—cars, clothing,

The fleshed heat of the neighborhood streets
Marking our bolt through adolescence.

By then I'd been hauled to so many viewings
Flowers meant only those overblown,

About-to-perish wreaths, their scents as cloying
As the handkerchiefs my aunts kept pursed.

iii.

It was cattails that saved me, and pampas grass,
The milled combs of the teasel.

Discovering their India-inked calligraphies,
It was weeds that brought me back.

I drew them once myself on rice paper:
Wet, black, blots and lines. We'd been taught

Drawing meant marks on paper, nothing more.
And yet the ink was now leafing before me.

iv.

My wife breezed in from her meadows one day
With the billowing armful she'd cut,

Then set fanning in the corner of the room—
Zen stalks, Zen plumes—*wild* the root word

Branching into each wilderness flower.
A whole life I'd spent missing the obvious.

Again today it's there staring me in the face:
Foxglove, ox-eye daisy, spotted touch-me-not.

ENDGAME IN AUGUST

Because ruin is what awaits us soon enough,

I've thought to offset the inevitable,
Putting in a second crop of snap beans,

A fourth of salad greens, hoeing up weeds
And ripping out so much perimeter ivy

Its ganglia will fire along my optic nerves

Tonight as I'm falling asleep. Poison ivy
Veining among the grape and runners

Of wild strawberry, I'm playing it safe
And gloved, remembering the summer

In Zionsville I was brought to this through love,

The flashpoint of my wife's allergies.
I knelt before the raspberries and lilac tree,

The scrawled, naked stalks of the privet,
Hoping to keep her from such ravishment,

My cuffed wrists prickling with sweat.

Days I spent, yanking out the mangy vines,
Trying to avoid the touch of that caustic

Which touches off eruptions from the skin.
Just as I'm doing now at another house,

Though what else here will ravish it?

WIDOWER

Today the museum seemed more a mausoleum.
Not the cached hoard of relics—

Stones with hackled edges,
Whale's teeth etched with sailing scenes—

But one dead thing after another placed on display,
Floors like drawers in a morgue.

*

Upholstered animals that once roamed for me
In back-dropped glades and veldts

Now were species from a kingdom lost to time,
Like the bones and fossils

Which were kinds of ruins to begin with,
And the Hall of Sculpture's plaster amputees.

*

"I just look like I'm lost," I'd said to the girl
Who'd asked if I needed directions,

But I blundered all the same upon jars of snakes
Coiled in their steeping waters,

The mauve sunken frogs that seemed skinless,
Their raw flesh sodden as pulp.

LARRY

He's not back from gathering leeches,
But he might well be, what with
The Wellingtons and walking stick,
The muck-colored layers of clothes.

Seeing me, he flashes the high-sign,
Or low—a palm-down, sweeping gesture,
Belt-level to the ground—
Happy as always to stop and talk.

Today about mushrooms, his bag
Stuffed full of their rust-specked caps
And spongy yellow pores, the spores
Like cracked black pepper.

He's found them fruiting beneath
A stand of pines, he tells me,
And the way he likes to serve them up,
Sautéed with wine and butter.

To his wife, he says, they're just fungus,
Who turns up her nose as well
At the wild garlic that he picks
As a garnish for his sandwiches.

Each fall hunters ask to access his acres,
Knowing his taste for the venison

Permission fetches to his table
In a tribute of steaks and roasts.

Not for him, any refusal of the edible gifts
Of this world. Nor, for that matter,
Anything that smacks of the Lake Poet's
"Hope that is unwilling to be fed."

TEASEL

Late summer, waiting for rain,
The light sea-green and backlit
In the understory of the leaves,

The little grotto of light
Which looks cool and sheltered
As the inside of a jewel.

Even the brown furze of lawn grass
Is drawing the promise of water
Into its nap, the teasel glowing

Brindle alongside the roads.
It's time again, nearing the start
Of autumn and the birthday

I'd thought I might never reach,
To begin relearning just what I know:
That anger is a kind of sorrow,

That you have to sit still,
That the white flash there where
The tail feathers fan says *dove*,

And the five mournful syllables,
And the heart-shaped fire.
A few blown leaves drift past me,

First winds raining in the trees.
Now, the dust growing damper
Under the grass, I want to say

That the air feels like the cool fumes
Of witch-hazel wicking off the skin,
That the flesh is grass after all.

The exhaustions of August,
I remind myself, will again give way,
The teasel give way all winter,

A stiff burst on a stem.
Seeing it then I might even repeat
My prayer for the burning earth,

The dust in rising columns
And light like gusts of heat.
I might even walk out again

Around these streets,
Remembering the way the dry sky
Flashed and darkened, rain

Stripped me of that feeling
Of standing there squandered,
Futureless in the drought.

ARBORETUM

1. *Sweet Bay*

The bay tree, glossy in a lozenge of light slanting
Across the floorboards, flat leaves flaring,

The wand-like limbs angling upward
From the trunk.
                 The summer we returned

To find a world stricken with weeks of drought,
I cut it back to where I hoped it might

Quicken in sap-green sprouts, and have
Pruned the brisk plant since, tending bracts

And shoots, dividing the tangle of teeming
Roots.
             Why then, last night in my dream,

Should I see it on fire once more, but this time
In the antlers of a deer? *Stiff points of flame*

Where the oils burned off and the bare horn,
Sooted, budded in its flowering crown.

2. *Flowering Dogwood*

Early October, the red leaves of the dogwood
Burning in the rain—

                      tiers of vermilion

And terracotta, the "kidney-ore" known
As bloodstone, the deepening towards magenta …

So much color it's nearly impossible
To make out the outline of any single leaf

On the small tree beyond my window,
Cardinal and claret, burning as if encaustic.

Ornamental, because of the size,
Which is half-a-crown shy of the roof,

And because it seems to reside inside
Its surround of air—

                    a tree made for a tapestry.

Even though thornless, its berries are blood.
In spring rust bleeds into the blossoms.

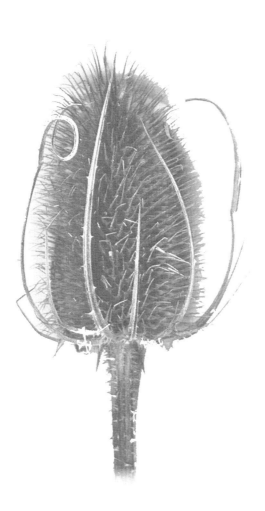

RIVER LIGHT

i.

Promontory, this stretch of road, come late October
When the river's back in sight through the trees.

Tug-boats, barges, the truss of the railway trestle
And flocked ridge beyond where Pittsburgh is notched.

They could see our *here* from space, the first astronauts,
The planet landmass riparian, marbled with blue,

The earth in its caul in the capsule window, the Giotto
Of the god's-eye view. And then the dead heavens.

ii.

Or take Andreas Cellarius, hard at work on another
Of his star-atlas maps, leafing gold plates in orbits,

Gilding the sun in its concentric, pre-Copernican track.
I like to think he centered the earth and modeled it

The way he did—solid as the root ball of a tree—
Because he knew that it alone was living. Like to think

The light takes on that color, here above the river,
By falling through branches of tamped gold leaf.

TWO SONGS

1. *Nocturne*

What woke me that night was not,
As I'd first thought, winds rattling
In the dead limbs of the trees,
But rather the clattering antlers
Of bucks in rut, jousting within the circle
The doe staked out, nervously
Along its rim—as though
Their business, too, were circumference,
And the moon's above them,
Rounding into the full, the stars
In their great wheeling chambers . . .

All of that darkness brought to bear
Upon the charmed space
Below my window where antlers
Formed the thorn of branches
At the heart of the contested world.
A conjunction like tumblers in a lock,
Or the ring at Stonehenge
During the equinox. You see,
We'd just moved here from the city
And regained the night sky,
And I woke to deer beside my wife.

2. Aubade

Out of a dream of helping my wife
Gain her footing on a sloping slab of granite,
I wake to find Skip James's spectral plaint
Playing inside my head—
If I ever get off this killing floor—
The light of late autumn filling the room,
Faint again this morning, and cold.
Can't find no heaven, he keens, and as if on cue
A few drops of rain streak the window
And fall from the branches outside.
Times are harder than ever been before.

In the dream I'd been fitting her shoe
Back onto a leg that ended at the ankle,
The smooth bones rounded like the haft of an axe.
Now I fit the covers back flat again
On the bed we slept in for fewer years
Than I ever would have guessed.
This month another birthday since her death
Will come and go, the days grow shorter
And dark. *Can't find no heaven,*
I don't care where they go. That lost, dreamy
Falsetto that's keening my aubade.

NEARING WINTER

i.

First light: tints of citron in the grapefruit which
Are otherwise the yellow of the kitchen walls.
First sill of white outside marking the horizon.

ii.

Throughout the night, stars and their stark anatomies.
In the morning, thistle and teasel and common dock.

iii.

How many autumns now have I found them gone
To froth, seeds flecked in the batting, or like this,
Reliquary and stiff, half-filled with night—milkweed
Whose udders are the color of the passing clouds.

iv.

Not cadmium or canary or the yellow ochre of weeds,
Peter Breughel, in your *Adoration of the Kings*.

v.

Or the fields above which that unlikely dancer,
The crow, hangs in an updraft like a torn black scrap,
Impossibly darkens, and slants off
As though riding the outward blossom of fire,
Afterimage the only ash left shimmering into the sky.

vi.

Approaching winter, my bride has changed—
White snow, white page—from adjective to noun.

AGAINST TRANSCENDENCE

i.

Jesus is the reason for the season
Proclaims my neighbor's bow-wrapped door,
Getting it exactly backwards again this year,
The winter solstice only weeks away:
Opaque slate skies, a daylong dusk in the drybrush
Of branches blurring in the woods.
Do you worship God or animals? asks a sticker
From the back of his pick-up truck.

Could he look down from the tomb of heaven,
Cotton Mather would be pleased
By the granite sky, the cold Old Testament comfort
Of the faith, and by the faithful,
Bedrock, salt-of-the-earth,
Hunkered down and ready to be raptured.

ii.

Winter nights enlarge the number of their hours
Wrote a poet with the name of a wildflower—

Of the White Campion which blooms at night,
And the Starry, petals ascending slender spines—

The frame of the sky flooded with constellations,
The tiny novae burning like bits of tungsten,

While here below, if air turn dry enough and cold,
There's the taste of metal that comes with snow.

iii.

Bare limbs and briars, the crosiers of weeds
Burred with their small spurred seeds.

AFTER

Beat, heart ... The earth
has not swallowed everything.
— MACHADO

i.

The first of the month the cactus gets watered.
The jade tree every other week. The tubs
Of dumb cane each Sunday. Intervals
Like octaves, halved along their cord of days.
Sometimes it's not so bad, teasing out rituals—
Fridays mean a trip to the supermarket—
Sometimes the rituals seem more like chores.
Sitting in traffic the other day I listened
To a voice on the radio claiming uncontested
Happiness was the goal: "You just choose it!"
Good-bye *Missa Solemnis*, I thought,
Good-bye "Cooling Board Blues." Sometimes,
Home in the flat light of late afternoon,
I can't even find my way into the music.

ii.

And sometimes, out of nowhere, there's a gift,
Like the dead tree blooming in the yard.
I'd thought its leafing was amazing enough,

But there it was, bridal in blossom—
The wild cherry toppled by winds last year,
Straight-lined alongside the garden. All summer
I'd mowed around it, admiring the luster
Of the cordovan bark, its bands of welted whirls,
How the fruit was now a windfall for the deer.
Leaves wick the sap from a blow-down, so
I'd figured the tree for the chainsaw this spring,
Already one year closer to seasoned,
And instead found it gowned in flowers.

iii.

Mornings at the laptop I float my words
On a river of light, white them out again.
The soft burrs of rust on the hillsides …
Whole hours, when it goes well, gone by.
Rust with its retinue of oxides, moth,
The effects of time, to waste away by idling.
Words to test on the current.
Words to sound out in turn.
Strange, this art in which we turn away
From others—*stipples of rust on the hillsides,*
The autumn raw sienna of the leaves—
In order to join them though our words.

iv.

Cordwood ricks, a lintel sky, the light
Stopping down toward the solstice. Otherwise
I sign petitions daily about Tar Sands
And Marcellus Shale, the parts-per-million
Of dominion, my pittance sent to outfits
Like Greenpeace, with which my wife
Had kept the faith. Across the road a lone deer
Browses among the picked-bare weeds,
Then works her way back into the thicket.
White scut. A dusk of drifting snowflakes.
The animal gleaning of knowledge from the air.

v.

The hawk from the aerie. Barbed feathers,
The Kyrie of its high, sky-piercing cry.
Though what I noticed this morning was stillness,
The missing wreath of wings at the feeder,
And the reason why: a sharp-shin in the tree,
Training the hard lens of his raptor's eye
On everything around him, including the wind
In the leaves. We kept a one-sided kind
Of company till he barely tensed and was gone
In flight, the small wings filling his absence.

vi.

Those old Taoist poets with their solitudes
And wine, how I envy them,
The way even their requiems were resolved
Into mountains and rivers and distance-
Smitten bells. Imagine practicing idleness
Beneath Incense-Burner Peak,
Gathering firewood before it grew too dark,
The winter sky turned glacial with stars.
Then, by midnight, your dregs-glazed cup.

vii.

Again today I unpack the last gifts I gave her:
The amethyst necklace and earrings,
And this little picket of cloth dolls from Peru,
Their stitched expressions and homespun clothes.
Even the T-shirt she wore to bed, a photograph
On its front of the street sign LOVE, relic
Of a vanished Pittsburgh. I ironed it into the fabric,
Wanting the inks of the image made fast.

viii.

Looking down onto the Monongahela,
Green against the rust-flecked haze of the trees,
I watch a lone tugboat freighting barges
Like quarter-acre tracts, the deckled wake

Widening upriver, and remember that *tract*
Also follows the gradual in the Mass,
And is sung in response, as I would this.

ix.

Nights spent trying to find her in my dreams,
In the pages of the notebook I filled outside
The ICU, those last days when they'd rush me
From the room: *keep—attend to—the warrants
Of her delight.* In the chickadee at my window,
An ink-brushed quickness canonical with song.

x.

Out of kneaded and let rise I time it,
Out of punched down and divided
I score the round tops with their pound signs,
The baking stone heating in the oven,
The cooling rack readied for the loaves.

xi.

This loneliness which comes at the end of day,
With the table and its single setting, the slow-
Motion hours, lights coming on in houses
Now visible in the distance through the trees.

xii.

Blind Willie McTell's "Cooling Board Blues,"
The hiss and scratch of time on vinyl—
Its craquelure—as the stylus rides the grooves.

xiii.

And that bird at the window, black-capped
And minim, bundling her quick bright grams.

xiv.

A little riff. A little braille above the fretboard.

WINTER CONCERT

The candle-in-the-dark of December.
We'd spent the evening listening to Coltrane

And Pharoah Sanders and (on vinyl)
Charles Lloyd, their scales and rasped falsettos,

The underblown fluttering codas
A kind of echolalia spun from the air,

The spirit almost vapor, almost the sound
You hear inside the shell.

Music, because we need to be somehow
Beside ourselves, body and soul,

Our feelings the acoustics of the room
Filled with those trellising arpeggios.

Then, on a whim, I unjacketed an album
Of recordings of humpbacked whales,

Their long, looping, beautifully-built solos
Rising out of the sounding depths,

Amazed I could have missed the obvious
Resemblances up till then—tonals,

Moans, flattened notes—all of it
The imperatives of the mammal breath

(How immense the distances of longing)
To convene within the darkness as song.

SAYING GOODBYE

Miles Davis famously gave up playing ballads
And with them that beautiful measured aching
He loved, he said, too much. The music
Would of course continue, but now without him
And those muted pining notes. Just as the elegy
Would survive my goodbyes, deleting poems
From that book for my wife, whose pages
Were grieving enough. Years later, they still unheal.

Who knew that Christmas would be our last?
We'd already lined up the surgery to unkink your spine—
Our sights were set on the nights after that,
Not the monitors that would measure your dying.
The first gift I gave you was a dress, to keep you
Safely under wraps, and only then to undress you.

IV

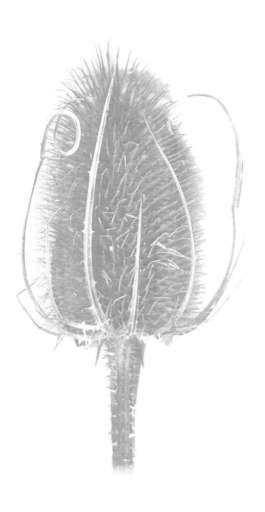

WILDFLOWERS (II)

i.

A weathered nubble on top of a stalk,
Still hinting this winter of umbels
White with Queen Anne's Lace—
The webbed threads all pinned in place—
And there below, the barest suggestion
Of a naked throat, of collarbones
Fanned against the tatting like wings.

ii.

The delicate needlework blossoms
Tattooed on the breasts of the artist
Whose performance piece startled me:
Radiant inked pigments spun from nubs.
It looked as if a camisole had left
Its traceries upon her, intaglio'd webs
Where the filaments of silk had clung.

iii.

Those compass flowers we drew
In school, all pivot points and petals,
The arcs, intersecting, blooming
Across the paper's corolla-strewn field.

Rays, when stemmed from the center,
Or patterned into parts of the cluster.
Spokes in the wheel-window rows.

SNOW DAYS

> *Anybody ever ready for real snow?*
> —William H. Gass

i.

A workweek's worth of weather:
Shoveling snow that's up to the knees
Except where it's drifted

Or been plowed into heaps—powder
On top of pack and nowhere to put it,
Branches snapped, black ice

On the roads. As though this is what
Is meant by *the dead of winter*,
The visible world all shelves and bergs,

The awning above my kitchen door
Now wedged on end before it
Like the fallen side of the sky.

ii.

Duration event, said the weatherman,
Forecasting its aftermath as well,
The excavated layers stacking up

Like solid blocks of scaffolding,
The surf coming tangent off the plows.
In Breughel, when it snows, the air

Seems stilled with the painstaking flakes
He's set falling in place, forming
The only consensus within that world.

As they do here in our own, centuries
After his Flemish-village Bethlehem,
The scrim of flurries in the air.

iii.

Like those flakes of cleanser, bleaching
Spots on the backs of fawns
In my friend's mother's watercolor,

The bisque-hued bodies set against
A landscape blank as this one—snow
The white of the paper taking shape

As Jersey barriers along the roads,
Cumulus on the spruces, caulk beads
Threading the overhead wires.

They're null as shadows in a negative,
Our yards the color of tarnish
Beneath the hard frost of the stars.

iv.

In the mills, with their mounds of gravel
And absorbent sand, we were taught
To run our shovels along the floor

Below the gradually collapsing slopes.
Snow comes down its cut banks
In stages till the blades scrape

Against the road, making that sound
Like mortar troweled from the board.
Days in a row we've tacked among

The cul-de-sacs we've quarried, corridors
Of blue cubic shadow where
The foundations have been laid bare.

ROAD SIGNS

1. *The Sphinx*

Lying on its side by the shoulder of the road:
The bald, eyeless head of a doll

Oxidized by smoke,
                    its child's brow rounded,
Its flesh *the hinge of salvation*

Which the catechism had quizzed us about.
Walking past the Baptist Church—

WAIT ON JESUS—I took the head at first
For the ball-joint of some major bone.

And then as something Pompeian,
Toppled from a pedestal,
                        but portending what—

The death of innocence or its persistence?
The flesh, we'd been taught, is what gets left,

A lopped outstaring remnant
Rolled off to the side like the stone.

2. The Man Who Was Mistaken for a Deer

Road kill, actually, heaped beside the highway,
As if in death he'd grown miraculous—

At least for the mistaken commuters—
A tale out of Ovid,

                     or set on the road to Damascus.

Either way, he suffered his sea-change
And season until that shape morphed back

Into his frozen, frost-laced remains,
No longer crowned with creation.

I keep seeing him at night, out alone,
Walking along the side of the road,

His shadow suddenly leaping in the headlights.
We shall not all sleep, said the Apostle,

but we shall all be changed.

                  All that time
And no one even reported he was missing.

FEEDING THE DEER

All day it's been mists and rain, small ponds forming
At the foot of the lot where the browse line leaves off,

The woods dissolving in a thatch of branches
Back to the side of the ridge. *Atmospheric perspective*,

I remember from Art History, rice-paper landscapes
Fading on scrolls, from branch to mountain to cloud.

Here it's simply emptiness—the vacant sky, the yard
With its absence of deer, both part of something

I've been trying to fill all winter. Now, still sopping
From my walk, I stand tossing apples off the deck,

Watching the way they roll to rest as though fallen
From the bough: a tumbled-down planetarium

Gleaming in the grass. They gladden a day I've spent
Pruning the dead leaves from house plants

And getting damp wood to burn, feeding the flames
With my wife's journals, their intimacies left intact.

I wonder if among them she mentioned her love
Of redness against crisp unblemished flesh, the sharp

Budding of taste on her tongue? I stare at those bright
Waxen planets and think how later deer will browse

Beneath the first evening stars, as if in the aisles
Of an orchard, amid windfall pitched there in the yard.

STACKING THE FIRE

1. *Wood Stove*

There was a house of straw, but it burned down.
There was a house of wood, of bricks.
But this one, corniced and squat, with its
Firedog legs and tracery-shaped grille,

Hunkers on the hearth like a floor safe—
The ash pan clamped in place just below
The grates, the ceramic-glass window
Softly candled with the first controlled burn.

A firebox cladded in metal, the lever-latched
Doors snugged shut. Out on the porch,
Bundled, bone-cold to the touch,
It sat as if waiting for its iron to be struck.

2. *Cord Wood*

Beside it, from the first cord I've stacked
In years, sit long split wedges
Of russet and buff, a fungus-crusted
Branch-end among them, round and black.

Pick-up sticks brought in from the cord
Chocked and cribbed out back, each layer

Ribbed on the one below as though
Thatched, a cut pile knit from the wood.

I watch kindling combust its pitch and resins
Until the logs seem spitted in flames—
Knots of fruit wood like burning coals,
The blossom-ends of apples in that bin.

CARDINAL, CARDINAL

i.

That berry brightness against the snow
And green of the mountain laurel,

Against the juncos, their foraging squall
In the bare weeds just below—

The cardinal insisting on distance,
At least between the males set back

In the atrium heart of the branches.
On the ground, pecking seeds,

Is another thing, though even here
They never seem remnants of any flock

Or to remain long as one of a pair,
Even though they're paired for life.

Unlike the juncos which are multiple
And burning black against the snow.

ii.

And you, brightness, out on a limb,
The focal point again of the landscape.

You're the first bird today at the feeder,
Perched in profile, plying seeds,

An eye to the structure of the light.
"*Cardinal*," the book says: "on which

something else hinges," like the doors
Of the air about your flight—

The air you've gladdened all winter
With those note-perfect solos

Taken up, note-for-note, by your mate.
Cardinal flower, virtue, number, point …

A bestower of gifts, the bird in the bush,
That in the hand would be the heartline.

LISTENING TO PHAROAH SANDERS:
A POEM FOR MY SON ON HIS BIRTHDAY

The name a gift from Sun Ra, fittingly enough
(Though Baraka contested the christening),
Plus the fact that he'd grown up in Arkansas
Above another ancient delta. Farrell Sanders
Back then, in Orval Faubus Little Rock.

Then his encampment in the alleys of Manhattan,
That opening in the Arkestra, and then,
Incredibly, playing with Coltrane on *Ascension*,
Then *Meditations*, where he shared the free-
Jazz lead. Then as part of the final quintet.

I thumbed through the record bins back then,
On the lookout for any Impulse! LPs,
Their exotic black and blaze-orange jackets
Promising a world of jeweled lights burning
Deep in swirls of brass. Ruby and Afro-Blue.

His years spent in the wilderness after that,
Winnowing the effects he'd been known for—
Slap-tongue, split reeds, overblowing—
Retracing his steps all the way back to melody
And its attendant stacks of chords,

The *Rejoice* LP, which is where I come in again,
One winter, mid-afternoon, the light of the air

Filled with snow, and on FM radio
Pharoah playing Coltrane's "Central Park West,"
The rising falling flakes of the notes.

He'd found the rich, warm, sonorous tone
He was after for that "churchy sound . . .
Sunday School type of feeling," voices choiring
Behind him, the bass the wood of the pews.
Then the gentlest quavering flurries at the end.

A few years later, when our son was born,
I'd play the album for him, winter evenings
After his bath before the woodstove,
His mother having carried him to the couch
Where he lay all ruddy and naked.

The highlifes especially, when they kicked into
The saxophone's frayed ecstatic riffs,
Would start his arms and legs pumping wildly.
Too young yet to even crawl, and here
His whole body would be jumping for joy.

STREET MARKET, FEBRUARY

Finally this morning the salt cod
Have made their cold passage back

To the sidewalk, out in front
Of the old Macaroni Company.

Stiff swimmers, split and flattened
The length of the spine,

They spill in stacks like cardboard
Or rough-cut lengths of shakes.

All Lent, I think, they'll be flaking
Upon the amazing plates

Of the faithful, having become
The sweet flesh once again.

*

Maybe that's why this morning
The vegetables at Sunseri's

Seem so voluptuous their skins
Can barely hold them?

Sleek-ribbed or swollen,
They look rubbed with a light

We're eager to feel the quick of,
Gathered here to gather food.

I edge among the crowded aisles,
Lifting lettuce from beds of ice,

Troves of olives out of vats,
Mushrooms flecked with earth.

*

On the road before us, a fork-lift
Blares its shrill insistent warnings,

Part of the fugue of traffic, shoppers,
And vendors hawking wares.

Clear to the end of Penn Avenue
There are bushels of fruit

In season, nuts in bins, tins
Of spices and imported teas—

The tumult for which we hunger
As much as food, as though for us

Cuisine meant just this medley
Of the senses being slaked.

V

APHASIA

Because the words get lost halfway,
He draws his finger across his throat
(A cold day, white sun, the sky gone gray)

And now comes out with *headache*,
Frowns, and then corrects himself: *stroke*.
Because the words get lost halfway

It's hard for him to have his say.
That familiar shrug when I nod I know.
A cold day, white sun, the sky gone gray . . .

There's nothing for it, but that we wait,
Huddled in a little dumb show
Because the words got lost halfway.

He's like a pitcher shaking signs away
To run through them again, but slowly:
Cold day, white sun, sky gone gray.

Then what there is of small talk plays
Itself out and we're back on our own,
Each farther parting step of the way.
A cold day, white sun, the sky gone gray.

WINTER THAW, MONONGAHELA RIVER, NEW HOMESTEAD, PENNSYLVANIA

i.

Now, after weeks full of ice and snow,
A sky the same dull side of the foil,

I look down onto the river and the stone,
Sun-lit stanchions of the bridge,

Their masonry mortared in layers
From the river's floor, light impastoed

On them as if with a palette-knife,
Light thinned where it glazes the water.

ii.

Wedged prows broke open the floes
On that river, keeping the channels clear,

A slow thaw working its way north
Past the mills, the trestles of that bridge

Cutoff now from either shore. Up here
Surveyors were busy laying out streets

For a Levittown that never got built:
Armorhill, Girder, Panel, Ingot …

iii.

Walking to work, winters, in the snow,
I'd thaw out in front of the ovens

The great slabs were plunged into.
I'd take my breaks out back by the river,

My breath on the air a visible cirrus,
And the smoke from my cigarettes.

Heat kept the mill roofs bare,
But the river was a freezing gray slurry.

iv.

This morning it's swollen with snowmelt
And rising as though fed by flood

Up the water levels of the stanchions,
Stone disappearing into its mirror,

One tier less making one tier more.
I used to watch the river change nightly

From liquid to metal to flame.
Now I chart water's light-glazed panes.

PLANT PROFILE

i.

Symplocarpus foetidus it's been christened
By the botanists, this Eastern Skunk Cabbage
Known also as Meadow, Clubfoot, and Swamp,
The many names of the one thing

Mustered to register its plenty, since all things
Are many at once, even this lowly,
Stink-leafed plant—Foetid Pothos, Polecat Weed—
That taps deeper into the earth each spring.

ii.

Above, where their thermals melted snow,
The mottled purple cap-and-bells
Sprout in the mudflats flanking the creek:

Pungent lanterns, floating wreaths,
Ratcheted by roots into damp home ground,
Having flowered, bearing down.

WORK SONG

i.

The gutter now emptied of its glut of leaves,
The storm door its cold panes of light,

While behind the house I've trimmed that pair
Of fallen, wind-sheared trees,
Their thicket grove of branches

Which more than once this winter,
Looking out, I mistook for a dark slanting rain.

I've picked up twigs and sheaths of bark,
Cut back the shocks of ornamental grasses
And barrowed them off.

Next, weather permitting, shovel and hoe,
I'll be milting the garden with compost.

ii.

Down there last year, I looked up to see
One molten bead of metal after another

Scudding above me till the whole swarm
Was building like a cloud. The next morning
I found bees on the maple, a coat of mail

Welded about the base of the bole
Where they massed their layers all week.

And though for most of that time
They seemed asleep in the heavy veins of nectar,
They left the soft bark gouged in places

To the green underneath, the tree oozing sap
As if a furious chain had cinched it fast.

iii.

Getting to the lawnmower at last—back-
Lapping the reel against the cutting bar,

Abrading the blades with paste—
I can't stop thinking about their humming,
Bristly little bodies, their terrific dream

Of smelting down the planet, summers,
Into the honeyed heart of its comb.

Or about honeywort, *the yellow-flowered
bee herb of Virgil,* which they source
For wax, walling the cells of the lattice.

I picture it blooming by the garden beds,
Bright with those dark molten beads.

LATE HOURS

In the meantime a single light is burning in the house
Beneath the last hard carbons of the winter stars,

And in my favorite copy of *Moby-Dick*—the spine
On this reading continuing to split—the *Pequod* is sailing
Toward the Line, her try-works unbattened, the whale
In that furnace darkness cut and minced and feeding
The flames that were "fed for a time with wood."

Today, sawdust showering the both of us like pollen,
My neighbor shouted over the two-stroke clamor
Of the chainsaw, "There's always more work,"
His brisk arcs sectioning the fallen trees into lengths
I'll let season, their capillary saps, then split into stacks
Of cordwood in which decades of light are stored.

From his post at the tiller of the midnight helm,
Ishmael is part-and-apart as usual, exile and namesake
And fated to survive as the epilogue of his own story.

The ship, like kindling, staved into chips.

EPILOGUE

We'd been underground all morning,
Clearing out a cellar whose ceiling
Barely cleared our heads, cobwebs

In the knob-and-tube wiring, junk
Stacked in places to the rafters,
Just as we'd found it when we moved in.

Now we were clearing a space
For all the things we didn't want
To do without completely, digging among

The mold of generations as though
Among the possible glories of the tomb,
Hauling up mattresses and tires,

Dead batteries, bed-springs whose spirals
Were like the circles trout make
Feeding at the surface of a stream—

The yard now littered with that clutter
Whose riddance meant we had room
At last to house our ruins in turn.

A PAIR FOR THE MALLARDS

1. *Water Garden: Lock & Dam*

Past the paired, wooden flights of perrons
Rotting on Pinky's now woodlotted lawn,
The flotsam of the homemade dam
Ponding his inch-deep stream,

I'm surprised today by mallards: the ripples
Of the wakes which he's made possible,
As though sponsoring their patterns.

Not consequence, I think, but dividend,
Watching the overlapping surface—
Current and birds—configure in a flux
That breasts against the lip of the brink.

Below it the halberd tips of irises spring
From the last lock along his hillside,
Dark terraced water fathomless to the eye.

2. *Westinghouse Memorial Pond*

A pond like a water clock, equinoctial,
Thirty feet across, filled again by the spigots
Budded in its bed, the spray of the fountain
In its center, lacy as a leafing bough.

And the gift of the birds to the season
And surface depth—to the vestibule
Of the setting—even though they were only
The puddle Mallards of the parks.

For two weeks now they've been at home,
Cross-hatching the waters with their laps,
Heads bottle-green and blazing out of black,
Or speckled, dun, but with that specula

On the wing-patches blue as causeways
They could have flown. Years ago, rural,
I drove back roads home, the light grown
Retinal, dark as ore, as the pond on which

I could hear the vast flocks settling in.
Here the light lies green on gold, leafing
Plaques and statue. Their way is wild
Who wheel from water straight into the sky.

CATHAY

i.

"The natural object," said Pound,
> "is always the *adequate* symbol."

For example: that whiff
> of rotten eggs I caught

The day after Easter,
> returning from my walk,

The pleached frazzled asphalt
> still splotchy with rain,

The first spikes of knotweed
> by the roadside, their rhubarb-

Reddish stalks in leaf
> that soon will overspread

The guardrail, the river
> still blue through the trees.

ii.

"So many things," the sage claimed,
> "to wound this heart,

There's not a single week
> that one would willingly repeat."

But I'd gladly have the week
> I drove leafy back roads

To buy seedlings for her garden—
> a stiff sprig of rosemary,

Slips of lavender and hyssop,
            fennel in feathery sprays—
The week in which
            we discovered bloodroot
In the laps of the trees,
            their wet petals pressing apart.

SPRING SEQUENCE

i.

So far all the perennials seem to have survived the winter,
The bed of fennel retrenching itself in one showery stem.

A mild run of days and I'm out here pulling up stakes,
Hoeing weeds whose roots reach down into frozen ground.

ii.

March thaw—the vultures on the updrafts like flakes of ash,
The forsythia in their little haze of yellows by the road.

Daffodils and lilacs. And just this morning, along the creek,
I saw skunk cabbage, the dark mottled flames of their spathes.

iii.

Again this year, underneath the awnings and latticed roofs,
The seedlings are exhalations of the potting soil set out in flats

At Chapon's. *Snow Crown, Jade Cross, Golden Summer*—
My cart fills up, at twilight, with the names of the earth.

iv.

As if the darkness spilled from crevices of sweet green light,
Two katydids, sheathed and translucent as leaves,

Trill from perches on my bedroom wall. I lie awake listening
To their bodies' crescendos. Tonight I don't have to sleep alone.

v.

Crossing the sets of train tracks back from beside the river,
I see how things go forward by twos: rails, ties, gravel beds,

The first of the ox-eyes now blooming along the roadsides,
The pincushion teasels within their collared whorl of spines.

vi.

Today I bedded the tomatoes in the shred excelsior of straw,
Spread side dressings of compost, pinched off any side-shoots.

The world one thing after another, soon it will be cucumbers.
"In the end," said Tu Fu, "I will carry a hoe."

Notes

"Specimen Days": The sculpture in the second section of the poem is by Bill Segunda.

"Two Songs": The lyrics in the aubade are from Skip James' "Hard Time Killing Floor Blues."

"Aphasia" is for Lee Hayes.

"Working in the Yard": The take on honeywort can be found in Henry Beston's *Herbs and the Earth* (Doubleday, 1973).

"Late Hours" is for Dan Drecksage.

ABOUT THE AUTHOR

PHOTO CREDIT: JANELLE BENDYCKI

ROBERT GIBB was born in the steel town of Homestead, Pennsylvania. He is the author of ten books of poetry, including *The Origins of Evening*, which was a National Poetry Series winner. Among his other awards are two National Endowment for the Arts Grants, seven Pennsylvania Council on the Arts grants, a Best American Poetry and a Pushcart Prize, the Camden Poetry Award, The Wildwood Poetry Prize, and *Prairie Schooner*'s Glenna Luschei and Strousse Awards. He lives on New Homestead Hill above the Monongahela River.